ROCKET!

Written by John Coldwell
Illustrated by Colin H Paine

HENDERSON
PUBLISHING PLC

Lauren and Ben had found a strange looking trampoline at the end of their garden.

"Who could have left it here?" wondered Ben.

"Perhaps there's an address label somewhere," suggested Lauren.

The two children searched around the trampoline.

"Here's a notice," cried Ben. "But it's not an address."

The two children stared at the label.

TO ENGAGE ULTRA-BOUNCE, INSERT KEY HERE.

"I wonder what Ultra-Bounce is," said Ben.

"The people who dumped the trampoline may have dropped the key, too," said Lauren. "Let's have a look."

Can you help Lauren and Ben find the hidden key?

"Here it is!" Ben shouted. Carefully, he pushed the key in and turned it. Nothing happened.

"Oh, well," said Lauren, disappointedly. "We may as well have a go on it anyway."

They climbed onto the edge of the trampoline.

"One, two, three... Jump!" They jumped into the middle of the trampoline and shot up into the air.

"Wow!" yelled Lauren. "This is like flying!"

"It *is* flying," cried Ben. "We've gone up, but we're not coming down."

"There's our street," said Lauren. "Quick! Wave! Someone's bound to notice us."

Look at the picture. Has anybody spotted Lauren and Ben?

ROCKET

Suddenly, there was a loud BOOM and a rocket zoomed into view.

"Where did that come from?" asked Ben, startled.

A large tube popped out of the rocket and pointed towards Ben and Lauren.

"It's like a giant vacuum cleaner," cried Lauren.

"And it's sucking us in!" shrieked Ben.

The two children came to a halt with a bump.

"It's dark in here," whispered Ben.

"We must be inside the rocket," said Lauren.

"I've found a switch," reported Ben. He gave it a tug and a light came on.

"It looks like some sort of control room," gasped Lauren.

A computer screen flashed before them. As they watched, a mysterious message appeared.

START PULL
WELCOME
RED ROCKET
TO LEVER
ABOARD THE

"What sort of a message is that?" muttered Ben.

"It's only muddled up," said Lauren. "We'll soon unscramble it."

Can you help Lauren and Ben unscramble the message?

"Okay," said Ben. "Let's see if it works."
He tugged the red lever.
At once, a humming noise began.

"We're moving," said Lauren excitedly.

"Yes," said Ben. "But where are we going?"

"I'll check on the viewing screen," said Lauren.
"Wow. It's like looking through a giant telescope."

"What can you see?" asked Ben.

"You're not going to like it," cried Lauren. "We are heading for a mass of asteroids. Quick! We'll have to steer through them, or we'll be smashed to pieces."

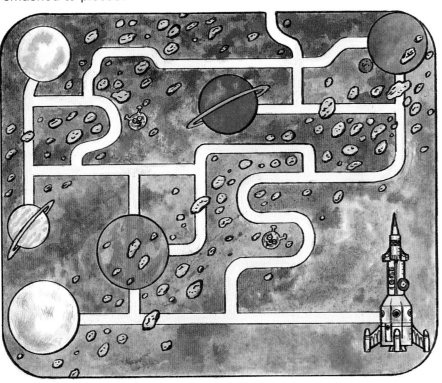

**Yikes! You must help Ben and Lauren to steer
a safe path through the asteroids!**

"That was close," sighed Ben.

At that moment, a door slid open and in trundled a robot.

"What does it want?" said Lauren. "And get it away from me!" The robot had begun to chase Lauren around the control room.

"Stand still," cried Ben. "I don't think it means you any harm."

Lauren stopped. So did the robot. The robot began to make clicking sounds. A roll of paper shot out of its front. Lauren eyed the robot suspiciously as she tore off the paper.

"It's a menu," she said. "But I don't think you are going to like the food."

The two children studied the menu.

MENU

snaeb
sgge
sregrub
dalas
spihc
segasuas

Can you decode the Martian menu and work out what Ben and Lauren will be eating?

"That was delicious," said Ben, patting his stomach.

"Emergency! Emergency!" blared a voice machine on the control desk. *"We are running short of fuel. Request stop at the next space fuel station."*

"I don't fancy running out of fuel in the middle of outer space," said Lauren. "We could be stuck here forever."

"But where is the next space fuel station?" asked Ben.

"First left after the planet Klypo," said the voice machine.

"But I can see so many planets on the viewing screen." moaned Lauren. "How do we know which one is Klypo?"

POGO
KLYM
ZEET
KLYPO
PLURG

A
B
C
D

"Here we are," said Ben, "a chart of the planets. If we compare these pictures with the planets we can see, we should easily be able to find Klypo."

Study the chart with Ben and Lauren. Which planet is Klypo?

Lauren and Ben steered the rocket left after Planet Klypo.

Lauren pointed. "And there's the space fuel station."

"It doesn't look like any garage on earth," said Ben.

Lauren steered the rocket through the main entrance.
A large sign overhead read:

> WARNING. USING THE WRONG FUEL COULD SERIOUSLY DAMAGE
> YOUR ROCKET. PLEASE MAKE CERTAIN THAT YOU ARE
> ENTERING THE CORRECT FUELLING BAY.

Beyond the sign were five tunnels. Over each tunnel was the
name of the fuel type.

"Oh, dear," said Ben. "Which tunnel should we take?"

"There must be a clue somewhere on the control board," said Lauren.

**Look at the control desk. Can you find a clue that will help
Ben and Lauren decide which fuel they need?**

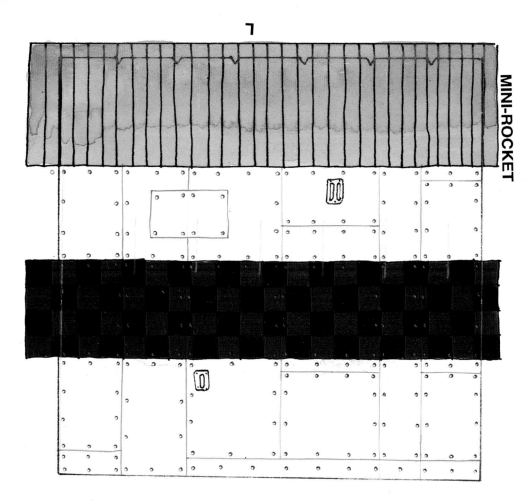

MINI-ROCKET

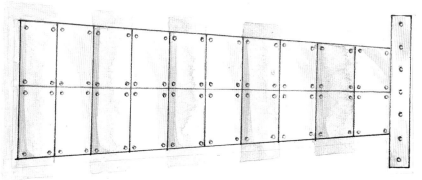

STAIRS

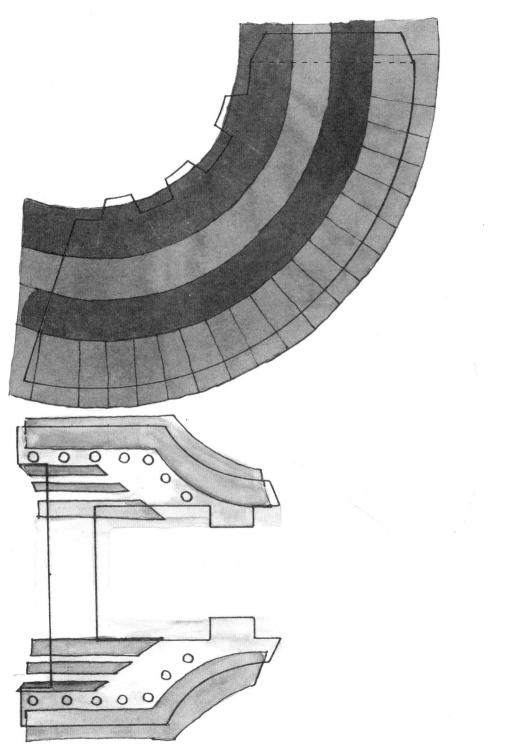

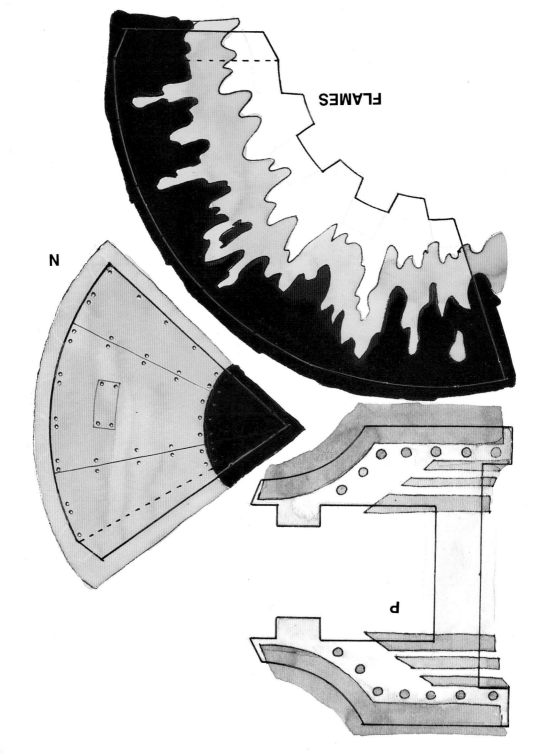

FLAMES

N

P

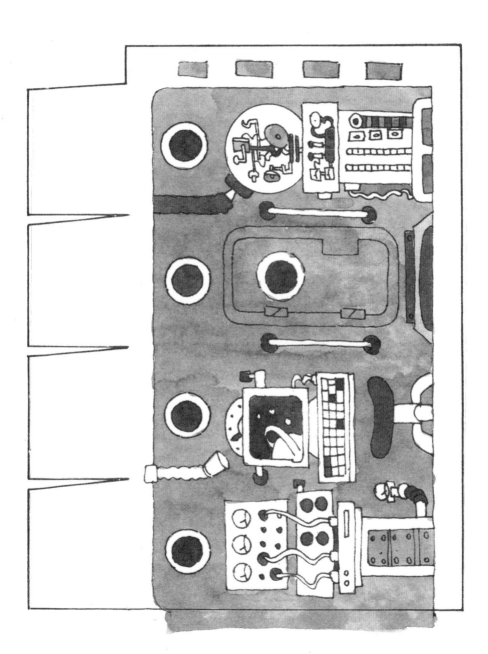

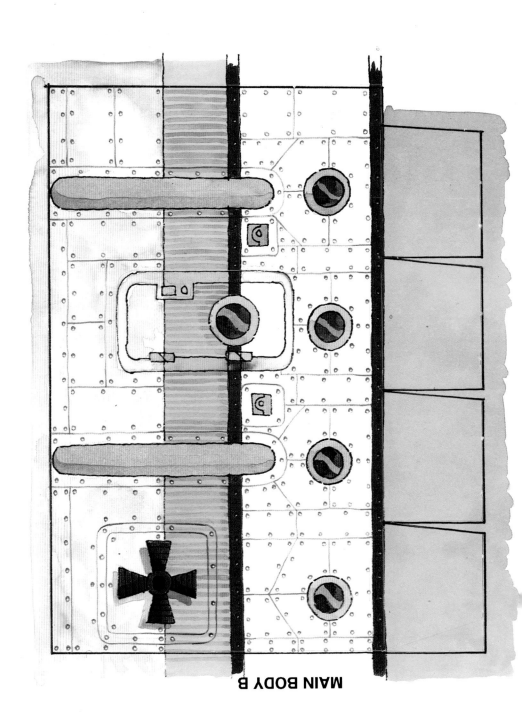

MAIN BODY B

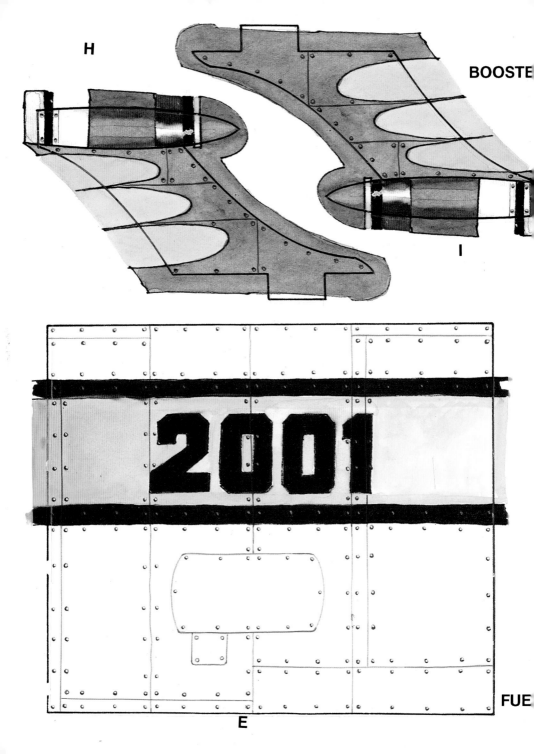

H

BOOSTE

I

2001

FUE

E

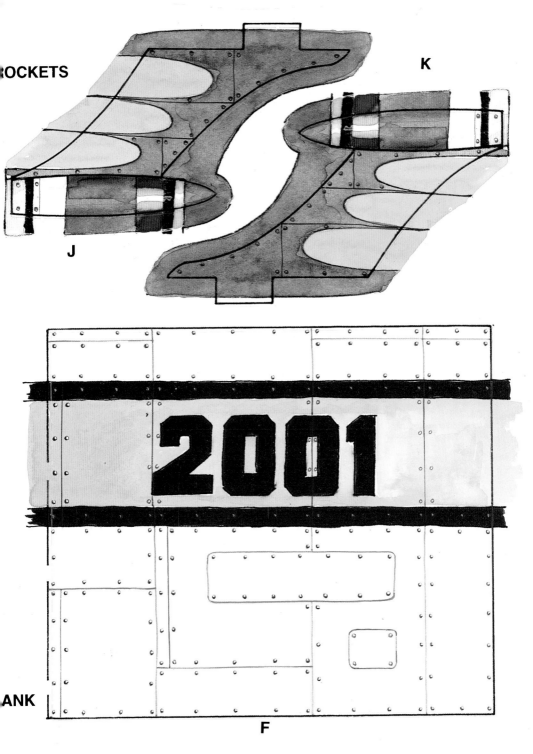

ROCKETS

K

J

2001

TANK

F

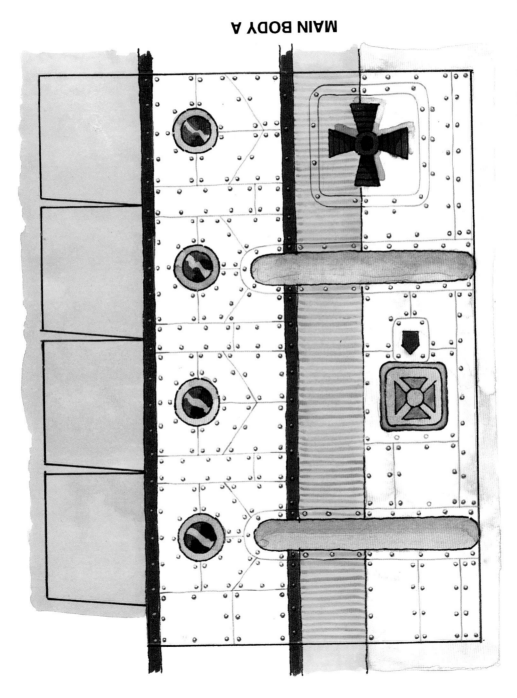

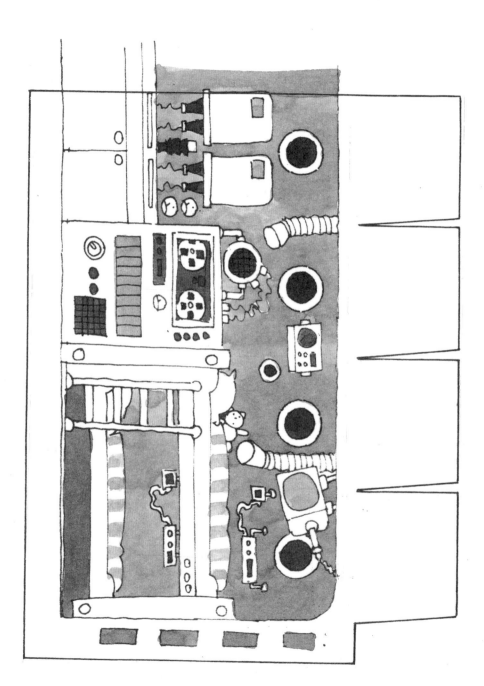

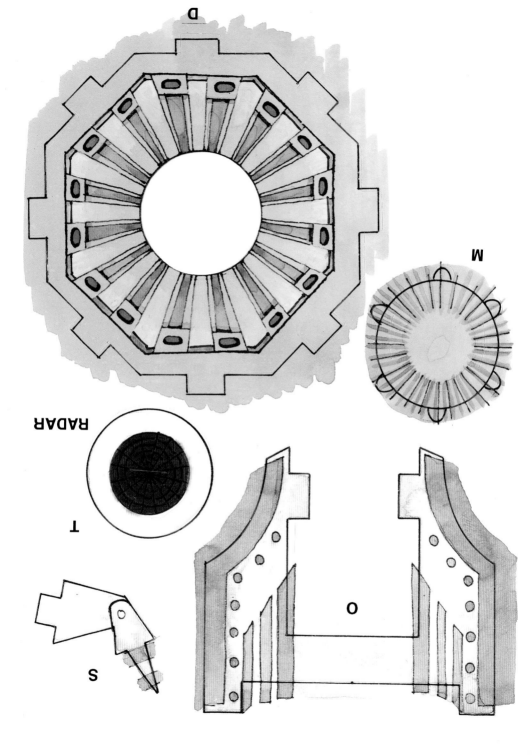

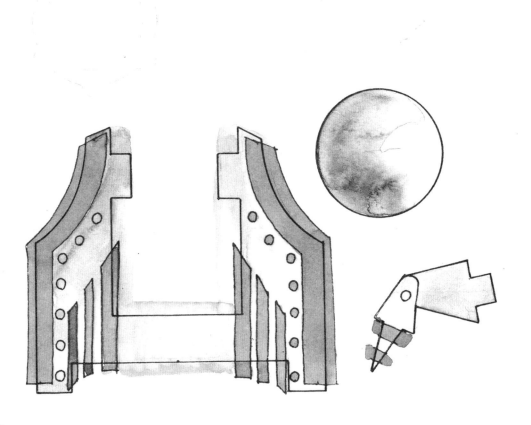

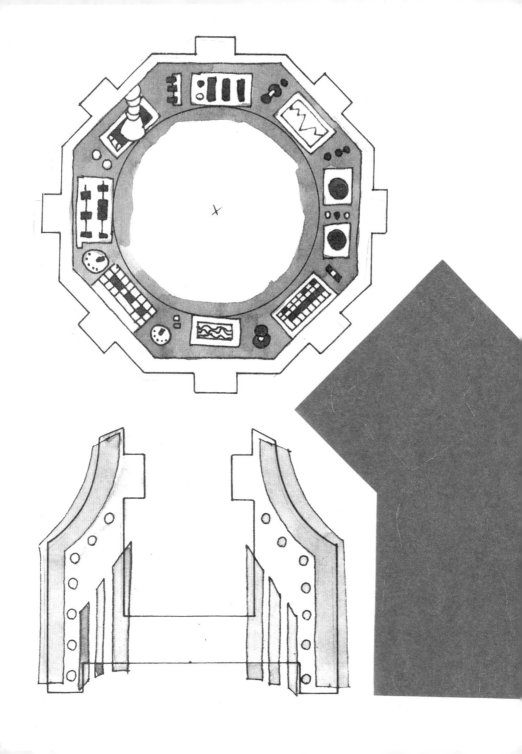

Lauren eased the rocket out of the fuel station. "Where to now?" she asked.

"I don't know," said Ben, "but there's a space creature waving to us from his rocket."

"Hi ya, Earthkids," said a voice on the radio. "I am The Intergalactic Garbage Grabber. My friends call me TIGG for short. It's my job to keep outer space clean. Hey, I challenge *you* to a garbage gathering competition. You can use the scoop on your rocket."

"Okay, TIGG," answered Lauren. "You're on."

Look through the viewing screen. How many pieces of space rubbish can you see?

"Hey," called TIGG from the radio. "That was a cool piece of collecting. I think you both deserve a drink. Follow me."

In a flash, TIGG and his rocket had disappeared.

"Where did he go?" said Lauren.

"I'll call him on the radio," said Ben. "TIGG. We can't find you."

"You Earthkids are just *so* slow," came TIGG's reply. "I am pulling into The Saturn Soda Bar."

"I can see it," replied Ben.

"Park your rocket behind mine," said TIGG.

Lauren began to lower their rocket into the rocket park.

"But we've never seen your rocket from behind," she said. "How do we know what it looks like?"

"Oh, man," groaned TIGG. "My rocket is the *only* one of its kind. You can't miss it."

Look carefully at the backs of the rockets in the rocket park. Which one of them is TIGG's?

It's not pink, it hasn't got a white stripe, it doesn't have seven holes in its tail.

"Hi, Earthkids," said TIGG. "I'll get the drinks."

At that moment, a robot slid between the two rockets.

"What-drinks-will-you-order?" enquired the robot.

"What have you got?" asked Ben.

The robot began to click and whir. A whole tray of different drinks appeared.

The robot spoke. "We-have-Neptune-Nightmare, Saturn-Sludge, Martian-Mess, Jupiter-Juice-and, today's-speciality, Venus-Venom."

"They all sound funny to me," said Ben.

"I'd try the Jupiter Juice," suggested TIGG.

"But all the straws are all twisted together." said Lauren. "How do we know which one leads to the Jupiter Juice?"

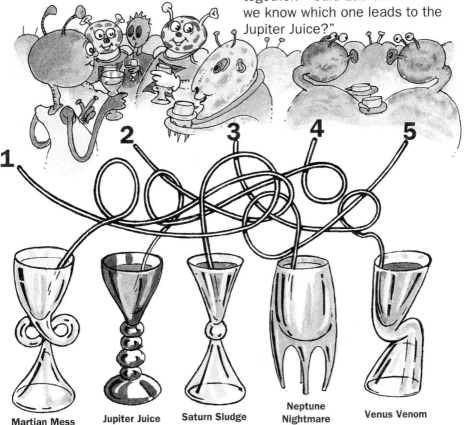

| 1 | 2 | 3 | 4 | 5 |

| Martian Mess | Jupiter Juice | Saturn Sludge | Neptune Nightmare | Venus Venom |

Which straw should Ben and Lauren suck to sip the Jupiter Juice?

"Mmm, I wish they sold Jupiter Juice on Earth," sighed Lauren.

Suddenly, a blue light began to flash above the door of their rocket.

"Uh-oh," said TIGG. "Looks like you've got trouble. Sorry I can't stop, but I got garbage to grab and planets to polish."

Ben and Lauren raced back into the rocket.

"Air quality is poor," crackled the voice machine. *"Suggest you change the filters at once."*

They flew into action. "I've found the filter box," shouted Ben as he pulled back the cover.

"And here's a set of replacements," gasped Lauren.

"But which filter goes where?" asked Ben.

Look carefully at the filters. Can you help Lauren and Ben decide where they should go?

"I think that we ought to be heading for home," said Lauren.

"Yes," agreed Ben. "But which way is home? What we need are some maps."

Ben searched around the control room.

"Look," he cried. "There's a drawer here, marked Route Maps to Earth." He gave the drawer a gentle tug.

"The drawer's stuck," he puffed.

"Let me help," said Lauren. Together they pulled on the drawer. The drawer flew open. The maps went flying over the control room.

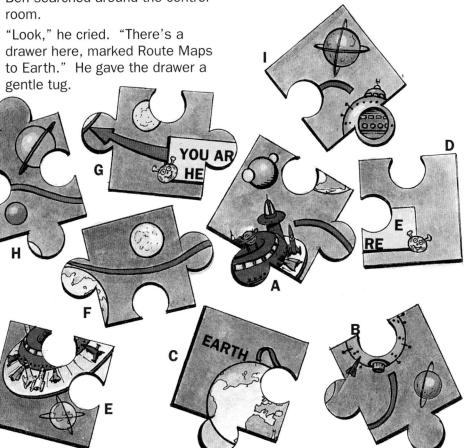

"Oh, no," sighed Ben. "Now we will have to put the maps back in order."

**Look at the maps with Ben and Lauren.
Can you sort them into the correct order?**

They soon had the rocket zooming back towards Earth.

"Flying a space rocket is easy," laughed Ben.

"And exciting," agreed Lauren.

"Well done, Lauren and Ben," said two voices.

Lauren and Ben spun around. There, standing in front of them, were two little creatures in spacesuits. "Do not be afraid," said the two space creatures. "We mean you no harm."

"My name is Zopton," continued one.

"I am Zapton," said the other.

Ben and Lauren smiled in a puzzled way.

"What's the matter?" asked the two space creatures.

"I beg your pardon," said Ben. "But you two look identical to me. How do we tell you apart?"

"Identical!" scoffed the two space creatures. "Not at all! Look at us very carefully and you will see plenty of differences."

Surely _you_ can spot the differences between Zopton and Zapton!

"There's our garden!" shouted Lauren, excitedly.

The two children gently landed the rocket between the shed and the garage. The children were glad to be back on Earth. Zopton and Zapton were delighted.

"You see," explained Zopton, "our planet has been trying to find out if Earth children were clever enough to fly our rockets."

"We have been observing you all day," said Zapton. "And you have passed all our tests."

"We can hardly wait to report back to our planet," added Zapton.

"In honour of this," continued Zopton, "we would like to present you with a special certificate."

Ben and Lauren stepped forward and shook hands with the two space creatures.

They looked at the certificate.

"Is this written in Martian?" asked Ben.

"No," laughed Zapton. "Hold it up to one of your Earth mirrors."

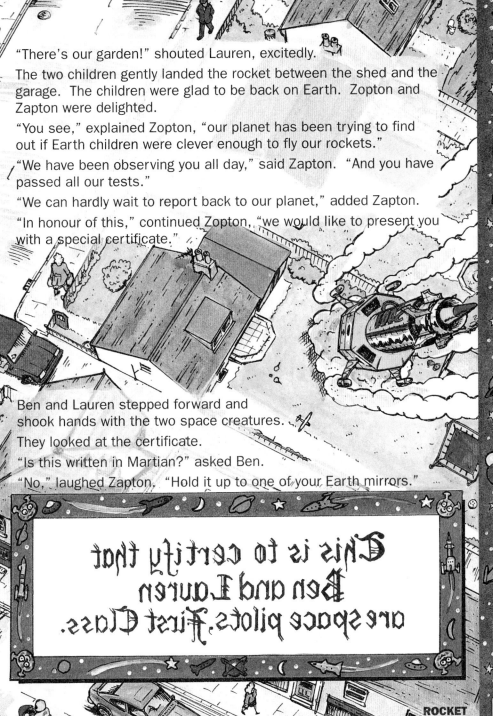

This is to certify that
Ben and Lauren
are space pilots, First Class.

Lauren and Ben waved goodbye to Zapton and Zopton. The rocket disappeared into space.

"Come on," said Ben. "I'm ready for tea."

"A pity there's no Jupiter Juice," giggled Lauren. They raced towards the house.

"Do you think that Zapton and Zopton really did watch everything we did in the rocket?" said Ben.

"I think they must have done," said Lauren.

Well, did they? Look back through the book for Zopton and Zapton hiding in every picture.

ANSWERS

The Hidden Key Inside the flower pot.

Who has spotted Lauren and Ben? The man loading his van has spotted them.

Computer Screen Message WELCOME ABOARD. TO START ROCKET, PULL THE RED LEVER.

Avoid the Asteroids!

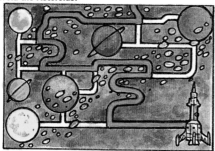

Martian Menu On tonight's menu are: beans (snaeb), eggs (sgge), burgers (sregrub), (salad) dalas, (chips) spihc and (sausages) segasuas. Yum, yum!

Which planet is Klypo? Planet D.

Which fuel? The rocket uses <+*> fuel.

Intergalactic Garbage Grabbing 10 pieces of rubbish.

TIGG's Rocket Rocket B.

Jupiter Juice Straw 4.

Fit the filters
 A3   B1   C4   D2

Route Maps to Earth
C, F, I
A, H, B
E, G, D

Spot the difference
The face patches, the gloves, the purse-belt and the buckle are each different.

Certificate
This is to certify that Lauren and Ben are space pilots, First Class.